The Me You Don't See by Sam Matthews
Published in Australia, 2020
Lilly Pilly Publishing
www.lillypillypublishing.com
lillypillypublishing@outlook.com

For children 5 +
ISBN: 978-0-6450186-0-8 (paperback)
ISBN: 978-0-6450186-1-5 (hardcover)

A catalogue record for this
work is available from the
National Library of Australia

The Me
You Don't See

by Sam Matthews
illustrated by Shez Kennington

To all the people in my life,
and my dog, Polo, who helps me become the best version of me.

Hi, my name is Sam, and I'm ten years old.
I am Autistic, which some people think is a disability,
but I think it's what makes me unique.

Every Autistic person has a different experience with life,
but this is mine.

Unless you understand it, you don't know why I do the things I do.
I wrote this book so others can understand Autistic children, and so
that Autistic children can understand themselves.

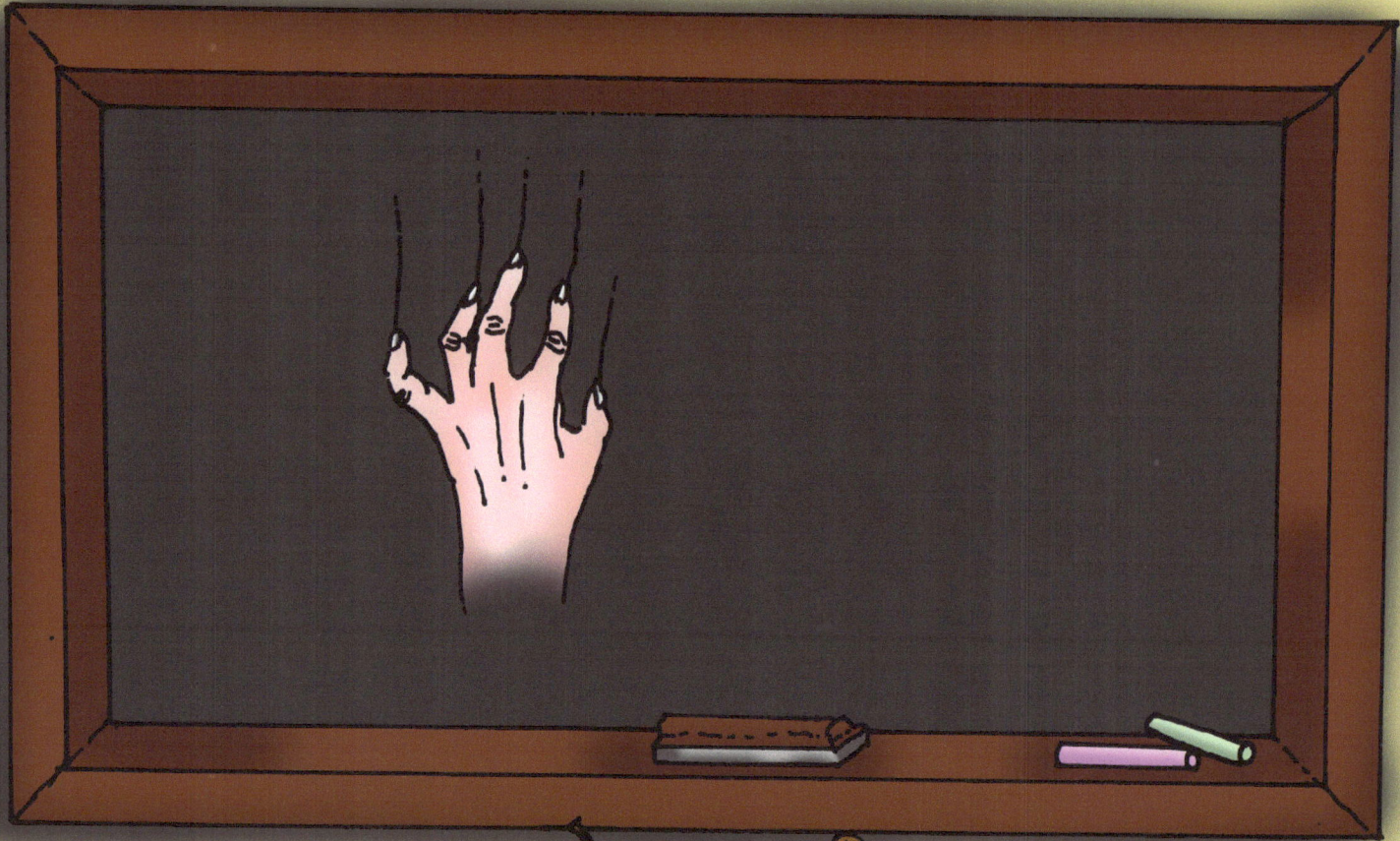

My body likes chewy and crunchy foods,
not soft foods like mashed potato and cooked vegetables.
They are tooooo squishy and make me feel yuck.

This is just the way my body is made, and sometimes I try
to be brave and eat new foods.

There are some materials that bags and clothes are made of
that I HATE touching! It reminds me of fingernails scratching
down a chalkboard.

I'm not being fussy, my body just can't stand it.

When people kiss me on the cheek, it makes me think
a snail is sliding across my face.

I hate it!

I also hate sunscreen, moisturiser and insect repellent.
They gross me out more than the way my mum gets
grossed out by road kill.

Yes, it's that gross!

My body hates toothpaste, hand soap or shampoo
because they are fluffy and feel weird.

I hate them so much that they make me feel
like running away to another city.

If I hear a loud noise, my brain gets **SHOCKED**
and my thoughts turn really, really fast.

I ask myself, "What's that?!?!"

Then I tell my brain, "It's probably nothing to worry about,
I'm going to be alright."

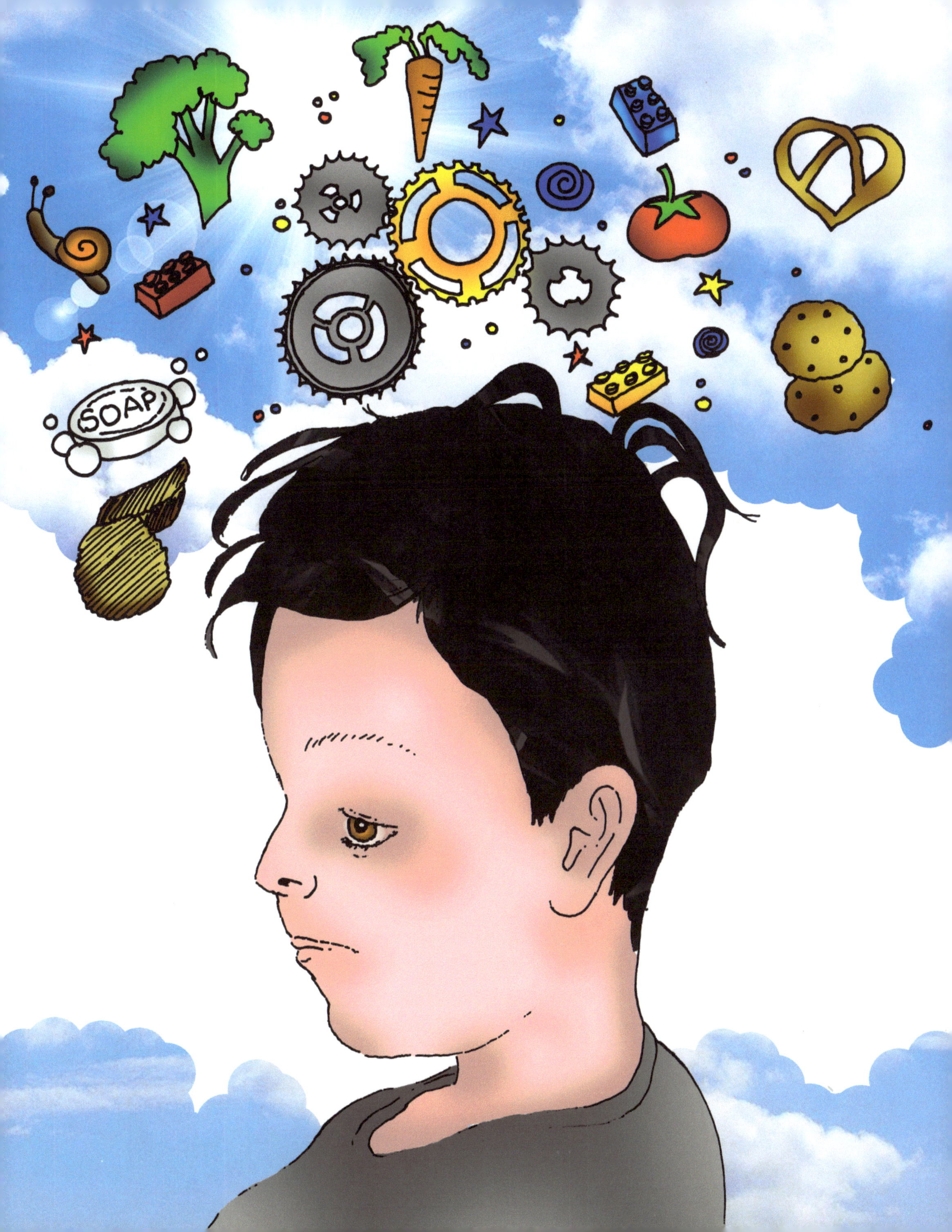
SOAP

After these experiences, my body feels REALLY stressed.

If I get on a swing, it helps my body calm down and
the thoughts in my brain go back to a medium speed.

Another thing that helps me when my body
has been through these hard experiences,
is playing with Lego.

Building with the muscles in my hands and using
my creative brain, calms me down.

It gives me a chance to turn off all the noises and movement
around me and just focus on me – wonderful me!

Some people say I am oppositional.
This means when people ask me to do something, I don't!
It seems like I'm ignoring them, and some people think
I'm disrespectful and uncooperative.

Actually, what is happening is, my brain needs more time
doing what it's doing to feel calmer. Then my brain can
take in a new step and follow what I've been asked to do.

My body may be feeling so stressed it feels unsafe.
I feel just like an echidna rolling up into a ball in those
situations. I can hear you, but my need to feel safe is bigger,
and so I can't do what you're asking.

When I'm asked to get an object like a plate,
I'll say, "But that's a bowl!"

I'm not trying to be a smarty pants,
I just like to be very specific about naming objects.

My new chore is to empty the bins. To me, it means exactly that, empty the bins.

To Mum, it means emptying the bins AND putting a new bin liner in the bin.

Sometimes I forget all the parts to my jobs. I feel very confused when Mum thinks I haven't done my job.

Every time I'm asked to do my chore, I need to know the exact things I have to do, or I can feel very angry because I think I'm finished, but Mum doesn't.

If I have been very active, sometimes it takes a
LOOOOOOONG time for my body to slow down.

I feel just like a Mustang GT on a never-ending highway.

When I need to slow down, I just read a book,
like the one you're holding in your hands right now.

If I've had lots of stressful experiences in my day,
I get restless at night and I can't go to sleep.

If I use something heavy, like a weighted lap blanket, it really helps.

My brain tells my body that it's like I'm in
an enclosed space, that I'm protected and safe.

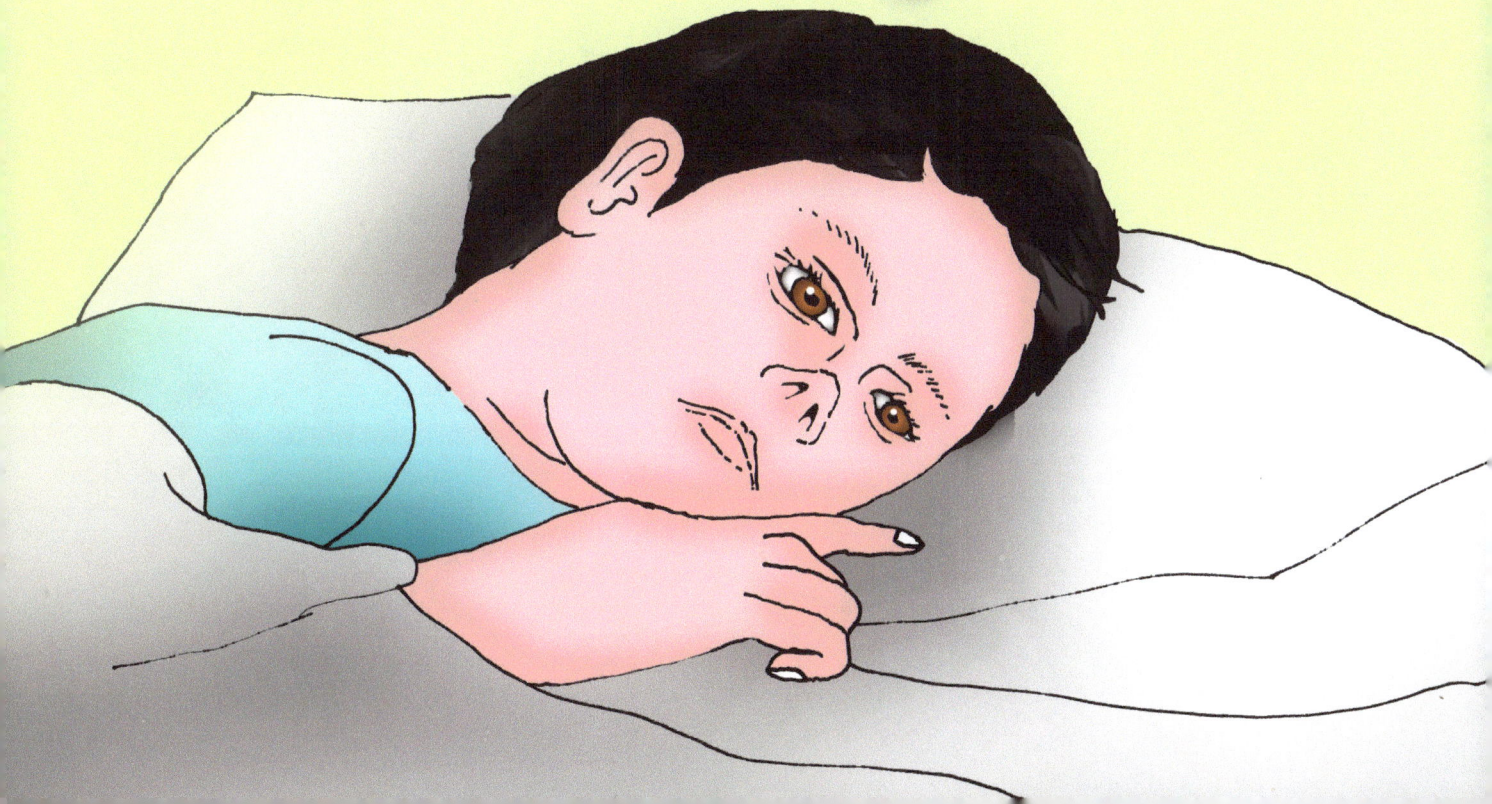

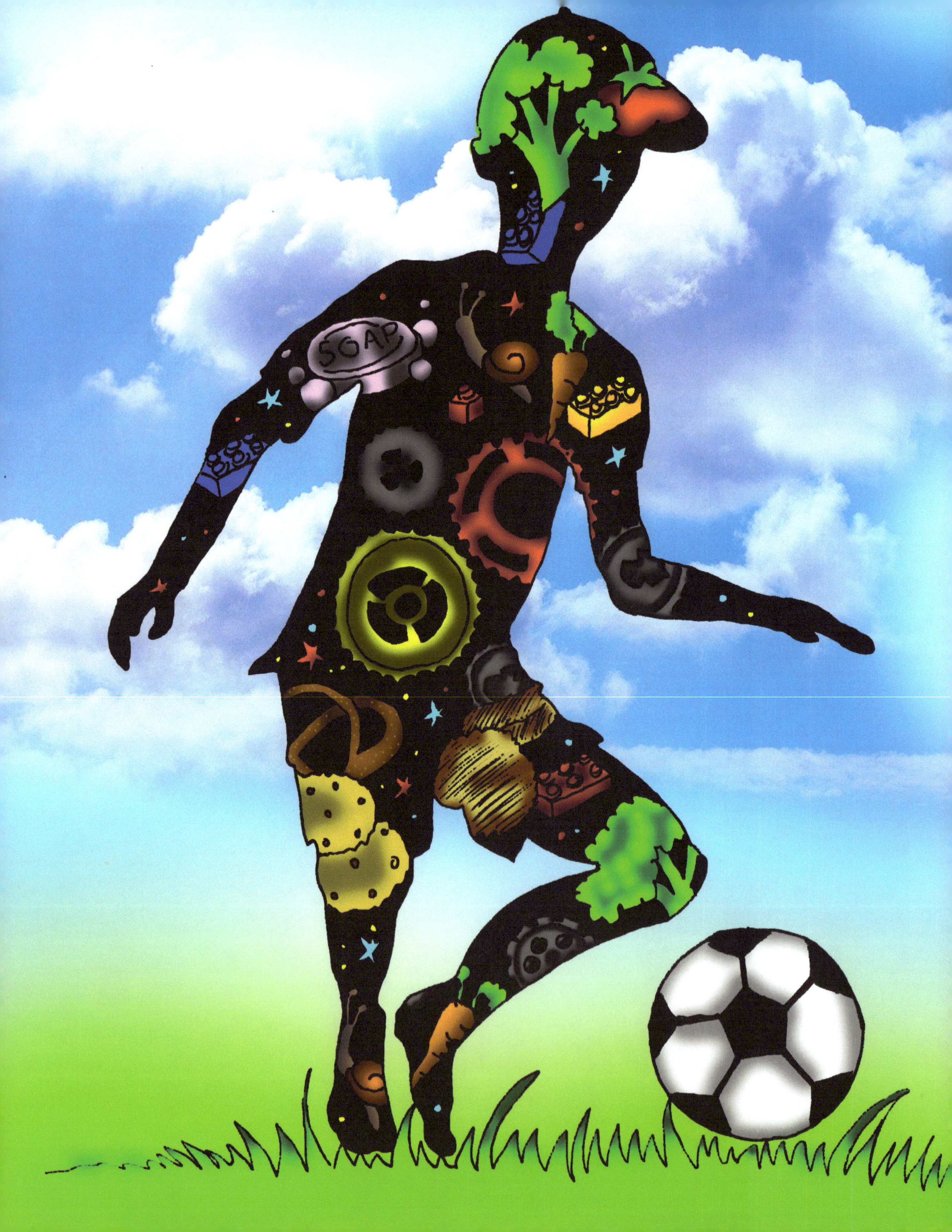
SOAP

Autism does look different on the inside to the outside,
and it is what makes me unique.

I like the way I am, and I'm learning about my body and brain all the time.

Autism is a GREAT ability to have because I'm creative, energetic and fun!

I look forward to an amazing future.

About Autism

Definition – *Autism Queensland*

"Autism Spectrum Disorder (ASD) is a spectrum condition which means that while all people with a diagnosis share certain difficulties, they can present in a variety of ways and to varying extents. ASD results from biological or neurological differences in the brain. The person on the spectrum may experience challenges in socialising and communicating with others."

For further details about Autism, visit *https://autismqld.com.au/page/what-is-autism*

Acknowledgements

Dr Rachana Dahiya (MBBS; BSc (Hons); FRACP; PhD) – for noticing I am Autistic and leading us to people who could support me.

Marguerite Moir (B.Occ.Thy (Hons) and *Sophie Bowen* (MOccThySt.; BHlthSc) – for recognising that I also have a Sensory Processing Disorder and helping my body work at it's very best.

Helen Kershaw (Dip SW.; MA non-directive Play Therapy; MAClinicalPsych) – for helping my brain (and my parents) understand the way I see life and be the best me I can be.

Andrea Gonzalez (Bachelor SW) – for taking me on adventures and challenging my thinking.

Ryan Isaiah (Support Worker) – for challenging me physically and teaching me about the Universe and life.

From Kathryn – the biggest thanks go to all these dedicated professionals who have educated me on the journey of raising a unique and amazing Autistic boy. Your wisdom, support and encouragement has meant that Sam will reach his full potential. You are the best!

My mum, Kathryn – for being supportive through my journey and helping me write this book.

Julieann Wallace – for believing in my dream, sharing her expertise and hours of her time.

Famous Autistic People*

Temple Grandin - Author and Autism advocate
Dary Hannah – Actress
Greta Thunberg – Environmental Activist
Dan Aykroyd – Comedic Actor
Susan Boyle – Britain's Got Talent Singer
Satoshi Tajiri – Creator of Nintendo's Pokemon

Autistic Speculation of Famous People*

Hans Christian Andersen - Author of "The Little Mermaid" and "The Ugly Duckling"
Albert Einstein - Scientist and Mathematician
Sir Isaac Newton - Mathematician, Astronomer & Physicist
Bill Gates - Founder of Microsoft
Steve Jobs - Founder of Apple (technology)
Wolfgang Amadeus Mozart - Musician
Tim Burton - American Director, Producer, Artist, Writer and Animator
Charles Richter - Seismologist
Lewis Carroll - Author of "Alice in Wonderland"

*For the purposes of this book, we have listed just a few known and speculated Autistic people. An internet search of "famous Autistic people" will provide you with many more names.

About the Author

Favourite Foods: all things sweet, especially white chocolate
Favourite Computer Game: Minecraft
Favourite Sport: Soccer
Favourite Activity: Parkour
Favourite Book: *The Me You Don't See*

www.ingramcontent.com/pod-product-compliance
Lightning Source LLC
Chambersburg PA
CBHW042014090426
42811CB00015B/1649